FEB 1 7 2014

J 152.4
HiC

$18.95

W9-CFV-530

Dealing with DEFEAT

Written by Kelli L. Hicks

Content Consultant
Taylor K. Barton, LPC
School Counselor

Bloomingdale
Public Library
101 Fairfield Way
Bloomingdale, IL 60108

Rourke
Educational Media

rourkeeducationalmedia.com

Scan for Related Titles
and Teacher Resources

© 2014 Rourke Educational Media

All rights reserved. No part of this book may be reproduced or utilized in any form or by any means, electronic or mechanical including photocopying, recording, or by any information storage and retrieval system without permission in writing from the publisher.

www.rourkeeducationalmedia.com

PHOTO CREDITS: Cover: © @ Robert Brown; Page 4, 5: © strickke; Page 6, 7: © Sergio Vila; Page 8: © Michael Krinke; Page 9: © kristian sekulic; Page 10: © Jstudio; Page 11: © Dan Harr; Page 12: © Steve Debenport, Associated Press; Page 13: © Mikkel William Nielsen; Page 14: © Curtis J. Morley; Page 15: © Rick Sargeant; Page 16: © Christopher Futcher; Page 17, 18: © kali9; Page 19: © Associated Press; Page 20: © Aviahuismanphotography; Page 21: © Photographerlondon; Page 22: © Dirima

Edited by Precious McKenzie

Cover and Interior Design by Tara Raymo

Library of Congress PCN Data

Dealing with Defeat / Kelli L. Hicks
(Social Skills)
ISBN 978-1-62169-902-6 (hard cover) (alk. paper)
ISBN 978-1-62169-797-8 (soft cover)
ISBN 978-1-62717-008-6 (e-Book)
Library of Congress Control Number: 2013937297

Rourke Educational Media
Printed in the United States of America,
North Mankato, Minnesota

Also Available as:

rourkeeducationalmedia.com

customersevice@rourkeeducationalmedia.com • PO Box 643328 Vero Beach, Florida 32964

TABLE OF CONTENTS

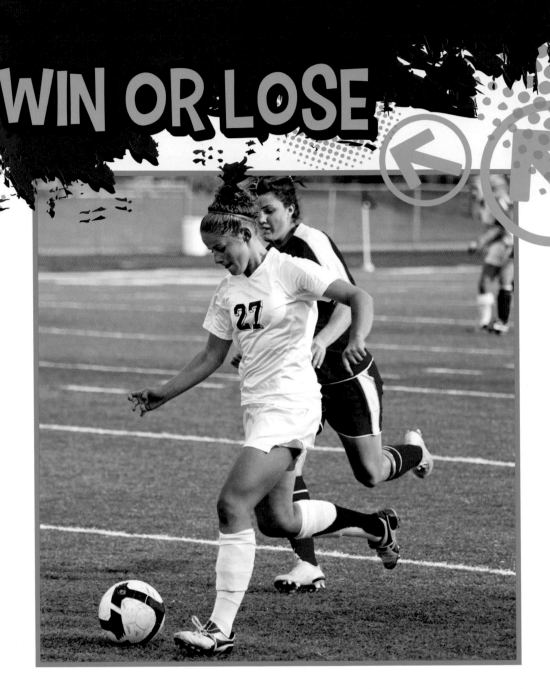

It's the final moments of the game. Your team needs one goal to make it to the **championship** tournament. Your teammate dribbles the ball past the defender and towards the goal. She pulls her foot back, eyes the back of the net, and kicks with all her might.

It looks good, then uh oh! The ball sails over the top of the goal. The whistle blows to end the game. How do you deal with **defeat**?

It can be really disappointing to lose, but stay in control of your **emotions** and be calm. Give yourself some time to think before you overreact.

Dealing with defeat is sometimes necessary outside the world of sports. Have you been a part of an election? Your posters were colorful and your speech told everyone of your good ideas, but someone else became the class president. It can be disappointing, but you can still find a way to help out at your school.

Recognize it for what it is…a defeat. It is a loss that might make you sad. It might even make you angry. But remember, everybody has to handle defeat at one time or another in their lives. It is **impossible** to win every time.

"Sportsmanship for me is when a guy walks off the court and you really can't tell whether he won or lost, when he carries himself with pride either way." — American Tennis Great Jim Courier

LEARN FROM LOSS

See defeat as a learning opportunity. Recognize what went wrong, and refocus your energy so you can fix the problem. If you figure out what happened, you can prevent it from happening again.

Madeleine L'Engle

Did you know that many authors' stories are rejected repeatedly before they get published? A *Wrinkle in Time* author Madeleine L'Engle was turned down 29 times before her book was published. Even Beatrix Potter and Dr. Seuss faced the disappointment of defeat by having their stories rejected, too.

Professional athletes watch videos from their games. They study their plays and look for ways to do better in the next game.

Avoid making excuses and try not to place **blame**.
Be sure to focus on the positive things that happened
in the game and confirm what you and your team did
well. Celebrate the things you have learned to do or the
things that you are now doing better than before.

It is important to look back at how you played your game and decide if you played well. Ask yourself these questions. Did I follow my coach's instructions? Were my teammates able to trust and rely on me? Am I proud of the effort I put forth? When you determine what you did well, you can come up with a plan for how to prepare for the next game.

Defeat is **temporary**. Figure out a plan for what to do the next time. Don't let the loss define who you are. Shake it off and move on. Part of moving on is planning for the future. What can you do to improve? Practice, of course!

Every person who is part of a team can help make the team better.

A WINNING ATTITUDE

Defeat is part of the process of learning your sport and understanding what to do to improve. Listen to your coaches and practice. You'll do better next time.

Jim Abbott knows how to overcome obstacles. He was born in 1967 without a right hand. Despite his disability, Jim learned to play baseball and became a pitcher for the University of Michigan. He later played in the major leagues from 1989-1999. Jim worked hard and dedicated himself to his sport. He said, "I worked very hard. I felt I could play the game. The only thing that could stop me was myself."

Be a good sport. The opportunity to play sports is a privilege. **Honor** and respect the game you play. Most importantly, respect yourself, your team, and the other players.

TRUE IN SCHOOL

If you lose a competition in school, the same advice applies. Be a good sport. Show respect for yourself and for others. Think of how well you did and what you can do better on the next time. Congratulate the winner.

Congratulate the winning team.
Tell the winning team they played well.

Learn from defeat. Trust in your teammates, and remember **victory** is in your future!

GLOSSARY

blame (BLAME): to find fault with or hold responsible

championship (CHAM-pee-uhn-ship): a contest or final game that determines which team is the overall winner

defeat (di-FEET): the act of being bested, losing

emotions (i-MOH-shuhnz): strong feelings

honor (AH-nur): to show great respect

impossible (im-PAH-suh-buhl): not able to happen

temporary (TEM-puh-rer-ee): not permanent, lasting for only a short time

victory (VIK-tur-ee): overcoming an opponent

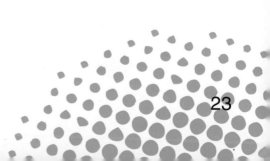

INDEX

WEBSITES TO VISIT

www.sikids.com

www.nflrush.com

www.exploratorium.edu/explore/staff_picks/sports_science

ABOUT THE AUTHOR

Kelli Hicks is a teacher and author who lives in Tampa, Florida, with her husband, her daughter Mackenzie, her son Barrett, and her golden retriever Gingerbread. Kelli is a soccer coach who knows all about the excitement of winning and the sorrow of defeat. She learns every week from her girls how to work as a team and how to support each other to overcome defeat. Go Rangers!

Meet The Author!
www.meetREMauthors.com

3 1531 00413 5163